TSUNAMIS

Earth's Power

David and Patricia Armentrout

Rourke
Publishing LLC
Vero Beach, Florida 32964

www.rourkepublishing.com

PHOTO CREDITS: Cover, pg 17 ©Getty Images; Title pg courtesy of U.S. Army/Staff Sgt. Aaron Allmon II; Pgs 5, 6, 9, 29 ©Photodisc, Inc.; Pg 6 inset ©Daniel Tan; Pg 10 inset ©Jordan Zupnik; Pgs 12, 13 ©DigitalGlobe; Pg 14 courtesy of the Philippine government; Pg 10 courtesy of USAID; Pgs 17 inset, 25 courtesy of the Department of Defense; Pg 18 courtesy of the U.S. Department of the Interior, U.S. Geological Survey/AVO/Michelle Coombs; Pg 21 courtesy of NASA; Pgs 22, 24, 25 inset, 26 courtesy of NOAA/Department of Commerce; Pg 26 inset ©Dave Gostisha

Title page: Thousands were missing and many more were left homeless in Indonesia after the 2004 tsunami.

Editor: Robert Stengard-Olliges

Cover and page design by Nicola Stratford

Library of Congress Cataloging-in-Publication Data

Armentrout, David, 1962-
Tsunamis / David and Patricia Armentrout.
    p. cm. -- (Earth's power)
 ISBN 1-60044-234-X (hardcover)
 ISBN 978-1-60044-343-5 (paperback)
 1. Tsunamis--Juvenile literature. I. Armentrout, Patricia, 1960- II. Title. III. Series: Armentrout, David, 1962- Earth's power.
GC221.5A76 2007
551.46'37--dc22

                        2006011221

Printed in the USA

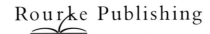

Rourke Publishing

www.rourkepublishing.com – sales@rourkepublishing.com
Post Office Box 3328, Vero Beach, FL 32964

TABLE OF CONTENTS

AN ACTIVE PLANET

Earth is a busy planet. The earth and sun provide all of the ingredients for life to thrive. But the earth is not always a gentle and forgiving home. Natural forces on earth make it an unpredictable place to live.

Weather is a natural force that affects plants and animals. Weather cannot be controlled, but it can be forecasted. Even deadly weather events such as hurricanes, tornadoes, and floods can often be predicted. Advance warning gives people a chance to prepare or escape. However, some forces of nature are much harder to predict and that makes them especially dangerous.

A surfer enjoys big waves along the California coast.

Tsunami evacuation route signs
point the way to safety.

TSUNAMI
EVACUATION
ROUTE

↑ 300m
เส้นทางหนี
คลื่นยักษ์

Coastal living has never been more popular.

AT RISK

The population in coastal communities around the world increases every year. In the United States, more than half of all Americans now live on or near the coast. Coastal communities have much to offer, but many residents do not realize they may be putting themselves at risk. What kind of risk? One of the most powerful and dangerous forces of nature, tsunamis! A tsunami is a wave, or series of waves caused by a sudden displacement of water in the sea. The greater the **displacement** of water, the larger the tsunami will be.

The term tsunami is a Japanese word meaning harbor wave.

TSUNAMI OR TIDAL WAVE?

Tsunamis are sometimes called tidal waves, but these waves have nothing to do with tides. Tides are caused by the gravitational pull of the sun and moon. Tides combine with wind and storms to produce normal waves on the sea, but they cannot generate tsunamis.

Undersea **earthquakes**, **landslides**, volcanic eruptions, and even **meteorite** impacts can cause tsunamis. A tsunami does not have to be big. Small ones, called micro-tsunamis, may be just a few inches high and are not usually dangerous. Large tsunamis may be over 100 feet high. These fearful waves are sometimes called mega-tsunamis.

Distant tsunamis travel great distances. They can affect areas thousands of miles from where they originate.

Local tsunamis affect much smaller areas, but can be just as dangerous. Landslides cause most local tsunamis.

Rough surf caused by wind.

A stone thrown into a lake sends bands of ripples over the water.

The 2004 Indian Ocean tsunami leveled low-lying coastal areas of Sumatra.

DANGEROUS

WAVES

When a tsunami is triggered, its waves rapidly move away from their source. Similar to the way ripples, or waves, move away from a rock thrown into a pool of water. However, tsunami waves can travel hundreds or thousands of miles.

The image most people have of a tsunami is of a towering wall of water crashing on shore. In reality, most tsunamis more closely resemble an incoming tide that rises higher and higher. Depending upon the coastline, a tsunami may rush inland a few feet or up to a mile or more.

11

Strangely enough, most tsunamis are hard to detect until they approach shallow waters near a coast. In the open sea where the water is deep, a tsunami may not be much higher than an ordinary wave. But it can travel at terrific speeds, 500 miles an hour or more. As it moves into shallow coastal waters, a tsunami's forward speed slows, but its height increases. Finally, the wave reaches land unleashing its full power on the shoreline.

© DigitalGlobe

Water from a tsunami covers the beach and floods the town of Kalutara, Sri Lanka.

12

A satellite image of Kalutara, Sri Lanka shows water receding after the first in a series of tsunami waves.

©DigitalGlobe

Tsunami

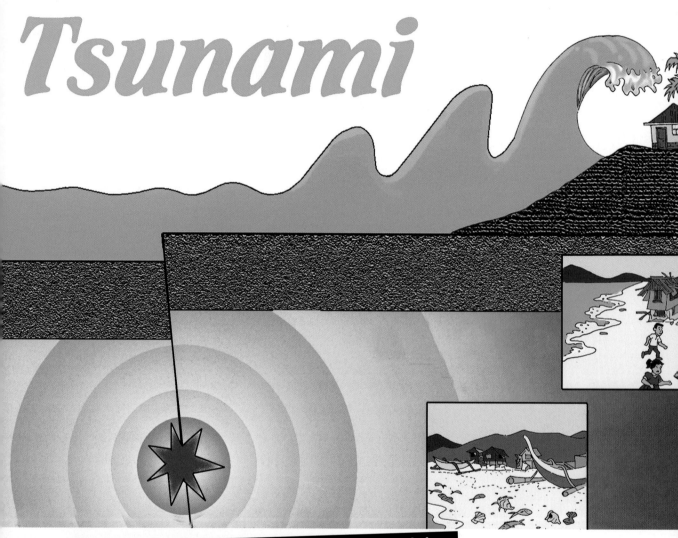

A tsunami warning poster distributed by the Philippine government.

EARTHQUAKES AND TSUNAMIS

Undersea earthquakes are the most common cause of tsunamis. Shifting rock inside the earth causes earthquakes. If an earthquake is strong enough, it can change the shape of the surface. Powerful undersea earthquakes can alter the shape of the seafloor in just seconds. This sudden movement of the seafloor displaces an enormous amount of water. The displaced water creates a tsunami.

<u>1964-Prince William Sound, Alaska:</u>

Alaskan residents who survived the strongest earthquake ever recorded in the United States must have been relieved. Many had let their guard down by the time the tsunamis rolled into the coast. Caused by the earthquake, the tsunami took many lives. The powerful waves killed more than 100 Alaskans.

THE 2004 INDIAN OCEAN TSUNAMI

On December 26, 2004, a monstrous tsunami swallowed up entire villages along the shores of the Indian Ocean. A massive undersea earthquake off the Indonesian island of Sumatra triggered the tsunami. Scientists that study earthquakes, called **seismologists**, reported that the earthquake lasted several minutes. Most earthquakes last only seconds. One of the deadliest disasters in modern times, the Indian Ocean tsunami caused major damage in Indonesia, Sri Lanka, India, Thailand, and other countries. It is believed that around 230,000 people died.

If there was a bright side to the disaster, it was in the way the world community responded. Dozens of nations sent money, relief supplies, and armies of rescue workers to aid the victims.

Survivors flock toward a helicopter carrying relief supplies.

A photographer shot this image as the first of several waves struck Thailand during the 2004 Indian Ocean tsunami. He escaped just before a larger wave destroyed the building.

Aid workers help to
rebuild a community
devastated by a tsunami.

An Alaskan volcano lets off a little steam.

18

VOLCANOES AND TSUNAMIS

Some volcanic eruptions create tsunamis. A volcano is a vent or crack in the earth's surface where hot **magma** and gas escape from deep inside the earth. Volcanoes may be quiet for hundreds of years and then suddenly erupt with colossal force. The explosive power of an eruption beneath the sea can cause tsunamis. Landslides triggered by a volcanic eruption can cause tsunamis, too.

KRAKATAU

One of the largest explosions in recorded history took place during a volcanic eruption on the small Island of Krakatau, Indonesia in 1883. The blast was many times more powerful than the largest nuclear bomb ever detonated. The sound of the explosion was heard more than 2,000 miles away. Scientists believe the eruption caused the volcano and much of the island to collapse into the sea.

Tsunamis caused by the collapsing volcano raced across the ocean. One of the tsunami waves rose to at least 140 feet, swamping nearby islands. One hundred and sixty five villages were swept away. More than 36,000 people were killed.

A satellite view of Anak Krakatau, or "child of Krakatau."

Anak Krakatau grew from the remains of the Krakatua volcano that collapsed in 1883.

A NOAA ship surveys an Alaskan bay.

1958 ALASKA TSUNAMI

A tsunami of frightening size happened in Lituya Bay, Alaska in 1958. The local tsunami was caused by a tremendous landslide of more than 90 million tons of rock that slid into the bay. The tsunami that followed reached 1720 feet (by comparison, the Empire State Building is 1250 feet tall) up the slope on the opposite side of the bay.

Two fishermen that had anchored their boat in the bay were killed. Fisherman aboard two other boats, anchored further away, amazingly survived by riding over the wave.

TSUNAMI WARNING!

Large tsunamis are too powerful to be stopped, but is it possible to predict them? In some cases, scientists can make useful predictions about where and when a tsunami might strike. The National Oceanic and Atmospheric Administration (NOAA) operates two tsunami warning centers—The Pacific Tsunami Warning Center (PTWC) in Hawaii and the West Coast and Alaska Tsunami Warning Center (WC/ATWC) in Alaska. Plans for a larger, global tsunami warning system are also being considered.

The Pacific Tsunami Warning Center in Ewa Beach, Hawaii.

Tsunami survivors search for any personal belongings they can salvage.

TSUNAMI HAZARD ZONE

IN CASE OF EARTHQUAKE, GO
TO HIGH GROUND OR INLAND

Planning and education will help save lives in case of a tsunami.

A tsunami warning buoy is launched in the Pacific Ocean.

Scientists at the centers monitor **seismographs** to detect undersea earthquakes. They also monitor ocean **buoys** and other instruments planted on the sea floor for signs that a tsunami is on the move. The tsunami warning centers notify regional and local authorities whenever a tsunami threatens.

Tsunamis are possible in just about any large body of water, but they are most common in the Pacific Ocean. Many Pacific coastal communities from California to Alaska and Hawaii have tsunami education programs and pre-planned evacuation routes.

1960-Chile:

In 1960, the largest earthquake ever recorded rocked South America. The quake was centered off the coast of Chile. Within 15 minutes, devastating tsunamis slammed into the Chilean coast destroying everything in their path. Thousands of people were killed. The retreating waves pulled many out to sea. Tsunami waves caused by the same quake struck Hawaii 15 hours later. Sixty-one people were killed in Hilo, Hawaii.

TAMING THE WAVE

One reason tsunamis are so dangerous is that they are not common events. People do not expect a tsunami as they might expect bad weather. Most people have never experienced a tsunami, so when faced with one, they are unsure how to react.

Tsunamis will always be a threat for people living on the coast. However, disasters like the one in the Indian Ocean in 2004 do not have to be so deadly. Early warning, education, and quick evacuation can save lives.

Most of us will never have to face a deadly tsunami.

GLOSSARY

buoys (BOO eez) — floating devices used to take measurements

displacement (dis PLAYS ment) — change in position

earthquakes (URTH kwayks) — sudden shaking of the earth caused by shifting rock inside the earth

landslides (LAND slidez) — sudden movement of earth and rock down a mountain or hill

magma (MAG muh) — melted rock below the earth's surface

meteorite (MEE tee ur rite) — piece of rock or metal that falls from space and lands on earth

seismographs (SIZE muh grafs) — instruments that detect and measure earthquakes

seismologists (size MAHL oh jists) — scientists who study earthquakes

FURTHER READING

Walker, Niki. *Tsunami Alert*.
   Crabtree Publishing Company, 2006.

Orme, David and Helen. *Tsunamis.* Children's Press, 2005.

Langley, Andrew. *Hurricanes, Tsunamis and other
   Natural Disasters.* Kingfisher, 2006.

WEBSITES TO VISIT

Howstuffworks
http://science.howstuffworks.com/tsunami.htm

FEMA For Kids
http://www.fema.gov/kids/tsunami.htm

National Geographic
http://www.nationalgeographic.com/ngkids/9610/kwave/

INDEX

ABOUT THE AUTHORS

David and Patricia Armentrout have written many nonfiction books for young readers. They have had several books published for primary school reading. The Armentrouts live in Cincinnati, Ohio, with their two children.